Teach Me How to Love:
Why What You Don't Know Will Hurt You!

Troy Spry

Copyright © 2015 by Troy Spry
Editor: Candice Davis & Karen C. Armstrong

All rights reserved. This book or any portion thereof may not be reproduced or used in any manner whatsoever without the express written permission of the publisher except for the use of brief quotations in a book review.

Printed in the United States of America

First Printing, 2015

ISBN 978-0-9964863-8-5

Xklusive Thoughts LLC

www.XklusiveThoughts.com

DEDICATION

This book is dedicated with all my love to my mother, Brenda Spry, who was my biggest cheerleader, source of inspiration, and my angel. You helped me to birth my passion, and I miss you and love you, mom. Rest in peace.

Dear Mom,

I miss you. I miss you so much that it hurts, but the difference is, this time, I can say it with no apologies. I think back to that first blog post I ever wrote, "A Mother's Love." Who knew the pain I felt from you dying would be the same thing that birthed this movement and this book?

Starting this journey of helping men and women to become better people and better mates, with the goal of building better relationships and better communities, has taught me so much about life and love. Truthfully though, I believe I've learned more about myself than anything.

I guess this was you and God working together to make sure I not only found my purpose, but that I was being held accountable in my own life and marriage as well. I guess you knew that with every blog post, every video, coaching session, seminar, speaking engagement, conversation party, or book, I would not only be speaking to others, but I would also be speaking to myself. Mom, you think you're so slick, but I can dig it.

When I look back and think about how great a mother you were, I realize you were an even better person. It was the spirit of selflessness you operated in that I actually made me more selfish. I watched you give so much of yourself to so many people that I honestly thought you were being taken advantage of.

I overcompensated by developing a "me, myself, and I" mentality. It wasn't until I did some serious self-reflection that I realized I was so hurt and angry that you left me that I missed the point.

I realized you weren't trying to teach me how to be selfish, but you were really trying to teach me how to love. You were teaching me to let my guard down and to open my heart. You were preparing me to be able to give the love it would take to love a wife and the children I would one day create.

Mom, I wish I could tell you I'm perfect, but I have to be honest and let you know I sometimes still struggle. Sometimes the selfish part of me still comes out, and sometimes I find myself trying to be mad so I don't have to open myself up to being loving.

The difference is now I'm conscious and I hear you whispering to me to open up, let go, and let love in. It's when I hear your voice that I can push past the control that comes with being selfish and open myself up to the love that comes with being selfless. Oh, and mom, I've got to confess letting go feels so good.

Learning how to love has been a process for me, I've come such a long way, and I just want to be able to help others do the same. Mom, I always admired you because you were in the classroom passionately teaching kids math and reading, but perhaps your best lesson was teaching me how to love so that I can now teach others.

CONTENTS

INTRODUCTION 1

HAPPILY EVER AFTER 5

BE "THE ONE" 8

IT'S NOT THEM—IT'S YOU 12

DON'T BELIEVE THE HYPE 17

CHOOSE WISELY, MY FRIENDS 22

REALITY CHECK FOR LADIES 28

A NEW LESSON FOR LADIES 38

REALITY CHECK FOR MEN 43

A NEW LESSON FOR MEN 49

SECURITY 55

PSEUDO-RELATIONSHIPS 61

DATING "POTENTIAL" 67

WHEN IT'S RIGHT, IT'S EASY 71

I CAN'T LET GO 75

TIME TO REFLECT—LET'S WORK 82

ACKNOWLEDGEMENTS

ABOUT THE AUTHOR

REFERENCES

INTRODUCTION

"Troy, I want to love her. I just don't know how."

This was one of the most profound statements I'd ever heard from a client, and it stuck to my ribs like some good old soul food. While a very simple statement, it speaks volumes. Of course, in typical Troy fashion, it got wheels turning in my mind (Lord, how I wish they would slow down sometimes!)

So the more I thought about this statement, the more it hit me that we are taught how to do a lot of things in our lives, but many of us aren't taught how to do the thing, which in my opinion, is the most important and fundamental thing in life. We are not taught how to love.

With the increase in broken families, an increase in selfish thinking, the microwave society we now live in, and the cherry on top, the popular phrase YOLO (you only live once) mentality, good examples of true love are few and far between. The truth of the matter is that we are just a sum of our experiences and the examples we've seen, and sometimes we end up following a lead that consistently takes us down the wrong roads.

I'm so grateful for my amazing audience—the people who follow the blogs and videos, join the LTD (lunchtime discussions) on social media, come to my events, and allow me to coach them—because I learn so much from them. Without my audience this place I call my platform, www.XklusiveThoughts.com, would not be impacting so many lives today. One thing I've learned for sure is that people still want love. They want healthy relationships; they want commitment; they want marriage. However, many are frustrated and confused, feeling like they're just spinning their wheels and getting nowhere fast.

Oh, and what you must understand is that these aren't just the single people who are looking for love; these are the people who are in relationships and marriages as well. **News Flash:** Just because someone is already in a relationship, doesn't mean it's a healthy one or that the person isn't still seeking answers on how to make it work. So where do the people who want to know how to love, how to date, and how to build healthy relationships go?

This is one of the reasons I became a relationship coach. It's one of the reasons I became so intrigued, took the classes, and why I began researching and investing in what it takes to create healthy relationships. My motivation came from a place of wanting us all to do and be better in life and in our relationships because I've seen how relationships can make or break a person and a family. The last thing we need is more broken people and families, so to all of you who have adopted me as your coach, I say thank you for entrusting me with that huge responsibility.

While I may not have all of the answers, I can guarantee you one thing. By the time you finish reading this book, you will be enlightened and will have learned something that gets you closer to knowing how to love. I've written hundreds of articles for well-known and reputable online sites and publications, like BlackandMarriedwithKids.com, DatingAdvice.com, DigitalRomanceInc.com, and celebrity matchmaker Paul C. Brunson's site PualCBrunson.com.

I've spoken at many events and have been featured on numerous panels, such as the ones on Huff Post Live. I've coached hundreds of clients and spent literally thousands of hours researching and learning about love and relationships, all so that I could do one thing: to fulfill the purpose God gave me through my mission:

"My Mission is to first inspire men and women to become better people so that they can become better mates, which will foster an environment for better relationships and ultimately help build better communities!

This mission is what encouraged me to build a platform, and it's why I've decided to write this book. This is for everyone who has ever wanted to love someone and wanted to be loved back. Now just in case you've never read any of my writing, I must warn you that I don't hold many punches. They don't call me a reality expert for no reason.

I believe honesty is the key to all things, and so I am extremely honest and vulnerable in my writing. It is my belief that you will only get something out of this book if you're willing to be honest and vulnerable as well. This isn't a "how to" book or a guide to knowing men or women. This is a "change your mindset" book. This book isn't exclusively for women or just for men, this book is for all people. So open your mind and your heart, and let's talk about learning how to love. Love is a journey, so come follow me.

Ride at your own risk, but you might just like where you end up!

HAPPILY EVER AFTER

I remember being in love back in the day and listening to the song "Happily Ever After," by Case, over and over and over again. That song, along with "Cupid," by 112, and "Gotta Be," by Jagged Edge. They made love seem so happy, so cool, so sweet, so kind, and so gentle. They made being in love sound fun and like we should all be falling in love. It sounded so real because it explained those butterflies I had in my stomach, and it felt like every song was about me and her.

The songs explained why I couldn't keep her off my mind and why all I wanted to do was talk to her on the phone all day, even if we were just listening to each other breathe. The music explained why I wanted to send beeper and pager codes of 143 (I love you) and why I wrote handwritten love letters to her every day.

I felt a lot of things about love at a young age, but something still didn't make sense to me. I couldn't understand how love and relationships were supposed to be all these beautiful things, but what I was seeing from my parents and other couples was so ugly. I was confused because one minute I thought they couldn't live without each other and the next minute I wanted to hide in my room because I couldn't take any more of the arguing.

I just didn't get it. I won't go into the details, but you get my point because some of you have thought the same thing at one time or another. Some of you have seen your parents or people close to you break up to make up, love to hate, or simply get up and walk away from each other. Others of you have never seen what a healthy relationship looks like because substance abuse or mental illness always had your parents in an alternative state of mind where they couldn't love.

Maybe your family looked like the Huxtables to the public, but was dysfunctional in private. Maybe you don't even realize what you've known all your life is really unhealthy dating or relationships, and it's become so normal to you that you really believe it's right. I call that "normalized dysfunction."

I say all that to say this: I've seen both sides of the coin. I've seen what a healthy relationship looks like as well as a dysfunctional one. I've been in healthy and happy relationships, but I've also been in a dysfunctional one. Currently, I'm in a committed and thriving marriage.

Through my experiences, the one thing I know to be true is that healthy relationships build you up, dysfunctional ones tear you down. If you ever want to experience next-level love or get to the next level in your life, you must know the difference. Knowing that difference lies in becoming empowered, and empowerment begins with you changing your mindset and changing what you allow into your life.

If you will continue to take this journey with me, you'll not only begin to change your mindset about dating and relationships, but you will put this book down feeling more empowered than ever. You'll also get some good tips on dating and how to give and

Teach Me How to Love: Why What You Don't Know Will Hurt You!

receive love better. Just keep reading because I promise you're about to get a lesson in love!

BE "THE ONE"

"Don't be so focused on finding the one; instead, focus on being the one!"

As I listened to a sermon by Pastor Steven Furtick of Elevation Church, that quote ignited a fire in my belly so hot that I went and recorded a video about it on my YouTube channel. The statement speaks volumes and I think it's the foundation of where we must start in this book. As I coach and interact with more people and host more discussions, I find a consistent trend in the world of dating and relationships. It's this trend of people doing the same thing over and over and expecting different results.

In other words, people keep choosing the same type of person or relationship and wondering why they keep ending up in the same types of situations. What I've realized is that many people can't get out of their own way, and it's not because they can't "find the one." It's because they aren't being "the one." They keep making the same decisions because they haven't taken time to self-reflect and figure out what work they need to do within so they can make better decisions, but also so that they can attract the right person.

Y'all know what this looks like. It looks like that friend who jumps from relationship to relationship with the same type of person, just a different name. It's the friend who comes to you every week complaining about her "bae" or her relationship, just to go back and continue to be an active participant in the dysfunction or drama. You know nothing is going to change, yet he or she keeps coming to you every week and acting like it will. It looks like you on the dating scene, constantly going to the same places, doing the same things with the same people, and yet expecting a different result, then you complain to your friends about how terrible dating is.

At some point, if we want things to change in our lives we have to engage in some self-reflection. What I've found through my coaching is, although self-reflection is the scariest thing, it is also the healthiest thing. I'm always amazed at the growth I see in my clients when they stop fighting me and stop trying to justify and explain their behavior.

Instead, they start to be honest with themselves, admit to the role they've played in their dating and relationship failures, and acknowledge what they should do differently. There is always a clear difference between the "he/she" clients and the "I" clients. Just so that's clear to you it sounds like this:

He/she client: "Troy, he was so wrong, and he led me on and mistreated me for years."

"I" client: "Troy, I realized that I allowed him to mistreat me for way too long because I thought he would change."

While the difference is subtle, the manifestation of that difference is enormous. One says: my life is in someone else's hands. The other says: my life is in my hands. You see I'm talking about mindset, folks!

Okay. Now that we've gotten that out of the way, let's talk a little more about "being the one." When I say that, I'm not insinuating that you need to be perfect, but I am saying that you need to be happy with who you are and what you stand for. You might just want to have an idea of where you want to go in your life. In other words, you need to have some vision! Why? Well, because if you have no vision, then you will just follow anyone, anywhere.

When you have a vision for your life, then you have a directed path, and the people who take you off that path will be easy to weed out. When I say you need to be happy with who you are, it's because you need to be sure that you are able to add value to someone else's life and you can't do that if you aren't happy being in your own skin. It is only when you feel you have value that you will seek someone of value. When you don't feel like you have value spiritually, physically, emotionally, or even financially, then it makes it a lot harder to want to go and seek a person who does. This is when a lot of settling takes place.

This reminds me of a client I had; let's just call her Stacy. Stacy was so hungry for love and for a relationship that she came to me asking me to "hook her up." Before she could go any further, I asked her about her past relationships. After going through a few of them, I quickly saw a pattern.

Every relationship was the same; it included her and some man with status and money and it always ended with her being cheated on or abused. I asked her why she thought she kept ending up in these types of relationships, and she simply said, "Well, at the time, I didn't think I could find anyone better."

See, what I didn't tell you is that while Stacy was a very attractive woman, attractiveness was about all she had going for her. She could pull five hundred likes on an Instagram picture in a matter of minutes. However, that was about the only thing she really liked about herself. Our coaching immediately went away from her "looking for the one," and I directed it towards her "becoming the one."

Within weeks, Stacy was back in college enrolled in a program studying business. She put together a plan that would help her get promoted at work, and she began a more serious spiritual journey and got back into church. In other words, she started adding value to her life.

Eventually, Stacy and I lost touch, but she emailed me a year later, and she seemed like she was on cloud nine. She told me she had gotten that promotion, she was doing great in school, and last but not least, she had found a man who treated her like a queen. The last sentence in her email read, "Thank you for encouraging me to be the one!"

Wow! I got a little emotional while typing that sentence because it fills me up knowing that when people put value in themselves, other people find value in them as well. I hope you got the foundational message of this chapter, and if not, here it is again. Developing a healthy relationship doesn't start with you finding the one; it starts with you being the one.

IT'S NOT THEM—IT'S YOU

When did everyone become so perfect? I need someone to answer that question for me because from what I've heard over the last few years, no one seems to have any issues with dating and relationships that are their fault…it's always everyone else's fault. The blame game is at its peak, while self-reflection and accountability are becoming non-existent.

On any given day, you can search Twitter, Instagram, and Facebook, and find millions of memes created by people blaming others for all that goes wrong in dating and relationships. While the likes add up and the retweets keep coming, there's one thing that's not happening. People aren't getting any better.

With that said, the second mindset I'll ask you to change as you read this book is your victim mentality. If you want to see real change and you want to become empowered as you date and build with a significant other, then you must first control what you can control. That control starts with you and within you—your standards, your mindset, and your behavior.

I know it's a lot more fun to sit around with your girlfriends drinking wine and talking about how terrible men are. But this time instead talk about the fact that you kept choosing those men. It's a lot more satisfying to say that you are alone because men are intimidated by you than it is to admit that you are alone because you just aren't that pleasant to be around.

It seems a lot cooler to chill with your homeboys and talk about how these girls aren't loyal than it is to talk about how you drove her into another man's arms. It's easier to say women just don't want a good guy than to admit you really aren't that different from any other player.

But y'all don't hear me though!

It's time that you get honest with yourself. Stop taking selfies if you don't really want to look at yourself. (See what I did there?) The truth of the matter is you have to take time to figure out what role you've played in your own dating struggles and failed relationships. With accountability comes empowerment, and once you're empowered you are more likely to make decisions in life and love that will better you instead of drag you down. It's time for you to be happy, and your happiness starts with you.

Why You Might Keep Falling Victim to Unhealthy Relationships

I find that so many times people are in bad relationships not because that's what they desire, but because someone has convinced them that's all they deserve. Maybe it was a family member, or an ex, or even a current mate, but for many, your worth has been compromised and your value has been depreciated in your own mind.

The most important ingredient in the recipe of developing healthy relationships and choosing wisely is self-worth. Thus the idea of lacking worth, value, and confidence is dangerous for a few reasons.

1) A lack of self-worth makes it easier for you to settle.

When you don't think you deserve the best, you will settle for subpar. You will settle for a piece of a dysfunctional relationship, instead of striving for a full healthy one.

2) You compromise your standards when you lack self-worth.

Instead of building a relationship, you will just accept what's given to you and fall for whoever shows you attention.

3) A lack of self-worth causes you to become resentful and bitter.

When we don't feel good about ourselves, we find it hard to be happy with someone else or even *for* someone else. This leads to many meaningless disagreements and a negative attitude. Neither of these is conducive to building healthy relationships.

4) A lack of self-worth makes you needy and insecure.

It's draining to be with someone who needs constant confirmation and it's annoying to have to entertain someone who is always fishing for compliments! The conversation usually goes something like this:

Her: Baby, do I look fat?
Him: No, baby, you look fine.
Her: Just fine?
Him: Baby you look beautiful.
Her: Stop lying. If you really thought I was beautiful you would have said that the first time. *You're just saying that now to shut me up!*
Him: I just can't win with you!

That's one frustrating conversation for a man!

5) You become a target for the wrong men when you lack self-worth.

A reliable recipe for ending up involved with a very controlling man is to present yourself with low value and self-worth. Some men prey on women with low self-esteem because they know they can break them down even more and take advantage of them. This never ends well.

My grandmother, mom, twin sister, and wife have taught me a lot and if there's one thing that I have grown to respect it's the value of a good woman! This is why it troubles me when I see so many women fall victim to unhealthy relationships. It very frequently stems back to a lack of self-value.

In the past, I've issued a call to action for men to become more accountable for how we treat our women, but that isn't where it starts. It starts within and with doing what it takes to feel valuable in your own eyes so you can be valuable in the eyes of others.

The best way to create a healthy relationship is to start with two healthy people. Make that the goal so that you can choose wisely, my friends! The fact is that when you feel better, you treat yourself better, and when you treat yourself better, others treat you better as well…because you won't allow or accept anything less!

DON'T BELIEVE THE HYPE

"Love is hard!"

"Love is supposed to hurt."

"We argue and fight so much because we are passionate!"

How many of you have ever heard some version of these statements? What's funny about these declarations is that someone who is in a dysfunctional relationship usually says them, and it's usually how he or she justifies allowing the relationship to remain dysfunctional.

In no way am I implying that love doesn't take effort, but I need you to understand that when it's right, it's easy! What do I mean by 'it's easy!' you ask? What I mean is that when it's the right person and the relationship is a healthy one, then the effort it takes to build and maintain that relationship comes with ease.

What I see happen so many times is that people allow themselves to exist in toxic and dysfunctional relationships because they have adopted the mindset that love is supposed to hurt. If you're the person who is being abused, mistreated, or cheated on, I am here to tell you the more you allow yourself to be mistreated now, the more damage you do to your future ability to love. If you don't believe me, step back and ask yourself

if you've experienced the following pattern or have seen someone experience it.
- You ignore all of the red flags and choose the wrong mate and then...
- You fall in love with Mr. or Mrs. Wrong and invest your all into him or her and then...
- You drain your emotional and spiritual bank trying to make something work, but your effort isn't reciprocated and then...
- Your heart ends up broken, and you find it hard to get over this person. You go back and forth for years because it's comfortable and convenient, and you've invested so much and then...
- You meet someone new who is great, but you find yourself guarded and unable to open yourself up to love or be loved. You feel lost and alone.

That five-step cycle happens to many people, and as a result they become emotionally paralyzed and empty. My point is you have to rid yourself of the mindset that love is supposed to be a difficult and an emotionally draining process. I often hear people say they are a "ride or die" person. My question back is always, "Why do you have to die though?" Love should breathe more life into you, not suck it out.

I'll leave you with two Merriam-Webster (2015) definitions of love and you tell me if it matches the "love hurts" or "love is supposed to be hard" mindset.

Love: Warm attachment, enthusiasm, or devotion; unselfish, loyal, and benevolent concern for the good of another

I don't know about you, but nowhere in those definitions do I see hurt, pain, or toxicity. What I do see is love includes being selfless, being connected, excited, as well as committed. Yes, when you love someone, those factors make you want to put in the effort it takes to make that person happy and to make the relationship work.

You are probably thinking, "Well Troy you make relationships sound easy, like they should be perfect." I'm so glad you brought that up!

There Is No Such Thing as a Perfect Relationship

Some days we see eye to eye,
At times we disagree,
But that's because we both accept
You're you . . . and I am me!

My wife and I recently celebrated our anniversary, and this passage came out of the card I gave her. While it is a simple passage, I believe it says a lot. One of the biggest reasons why marriages and relationships fall apart is because we get with people not for who they are, but for who we hoped they will be. It's almost as if we purchase someone "as is" and then want to return them for being "damaged!"

Sometimes our failure to truly embrace our partners for who they are keeps us from being able to love them at the highest level. Instead, we continue to wait for another person to show up. This is why so many marriages end with the following three phrases.

Marriage-ending phrase #1: "We grew apart."

People don't just grow apart; people just don't put in the effort it takes to stay connected and stay together. Often that's because you get frustrated with your mate's flaws while ignoring your mate's great qualities.

For example, instead of embracing the fact that he's a great provider and father, you focus on the fact that he sometimes leaves his pants in the middle of the bedroom floor. Instead of focusing on how much she supports you and how much she does for your family, you focus on the fact that she can sometimes be a little emotionally needy or the fact that she doesn't have the body of a fitness model.

When you focus on every negative thing about your mate and become less conscious of staying engaged, you lose connectivity and "grow apart." Simply put, if you don't want to grow apart, then grow together.

Marriage-ending phrase #2: "He (or she) changed."

Although as people we are always evolving there comes a time in life, usually after about the age of thirty, that the core of who we are is usually already established. This means that after age 30 people don't normally change much more in terms of their personalities, likes, and dislikes…the core of who they are.

One reason many people act as if their mate just did a flip-flop and "changed" is because during the dating phase the desire for the ring and the "happily ever after" blinded them from actually seeing the real person they were dating. That potential ring was so shiny that the glare covered up any of the flaws the suitor had or the baggage she brought into the relationship.

If you want to have more longevity in your relationships you have to take the time to truly get to know someone on the front end. You have to see how the person responds in multiple situations—under stress, through happiness, through highs, and through lows. You have to examine who people are in totality, not just who they are when things are hot and steamy. When you do this, you realize most people don't change but rather that being in a marriage just magnifies who they already are.

Marriage-ending phrase #3: "We fell out of love."

The romantic version of lust has been substituted for what love truly is. Love is a verb, an action word. It is expressed in what we do and how we serve one another. Most times when people say they fell out of love, what they've really done is fall out of lust. Suddenly the butterflies turn into gnats and the fireworks turn into dull flames, and as a result they want out.

They don't realize that if they seek to serve instead of being served and if they consciously make the decision to keep their mates happy, then even when the fireworks aren't there, the love will still remain. The action word "love" is what pushes you to put in the effort when it doesn't come as naturally as it used to. Falling out of love isn't an option when you don't want it to be.

There is no such thing as a perfect relationship, but we can make sure our relationships thrive when we accept people for who they are, focus on the things we love about them, and put in the effort to stay connected.

CHOOSE WISELY, MY FRIENDS

I don't know if you caught it or not, but I shared the following sentiment in the previous chapter. "Oftentimes one of the biggest reasons why relationships fall apart is because we get with the person not for who they are, but for who we hoped they would be." This brings about the need for us to have a serious discussion about dating and how to choose the right mate so you don't end up in those "love is hard" type relationships.

Ninety percent of creating healthy, sustainable relationships comes from choosing the right person. Too often we end up playing musical chairs with mates and putting ourselves on emotional rollercoasters because we don't slow down long enough to make better choices.

I had a client—let's just call her Lisa—who one day came to me for coaching. In our initial consultation she informed me that she had been in four different relationships in the last two years. I'm not great at math, but that's something like a new relationship every six months. You may be thinking, "Well, at least she doesn't have a problem getting anyone to commit to her. I can't find anyone serious about a relationship."

She finds her way into relationships, but what good is it doing her if she keeps relationship jumping because she keeps choosing the wrong person?

After further speaking with Lisa it was obvious she had no idea of what she truly wanted and needed in a mate. All she knew was that she liked the attention, the consistency, and the security of being with someone. Not to mention she liked sex, but with one consistent partner.

It's obvious that Lisa repeatedly rushed into relationships when she really needed to take some time, by herself, to do some self-inventory and some self-reflection. During her coaching, we took time to help Lisa identify what her core values were and what her deal-breakers were. Turns out that the guys she was choosing didn't share most of her values and had red flags, which should've been deal-breakers, all over the place.

For those of you wondering what a core value is and what a deal-breaker is, let me define them from my own personal dictionary first, and then I'll give you definitions from some of the bigwigs in academia.

Troy's definition of core values: What makes you who you are and what you need nurtured to be happy.

Therapist and Temple University instructor JoAnne White, PhD, (2005) states: "These are the things about yourself that are not likely to change. They are the tenets you grew up believing and that deep down inside still seem to fit into your life no matter what else changes."

Mercy College associate professor Gilda Carle, PhD, (2005) states: "When it comes to our most important and lasting relationships, it's similar core values that become the glue that cements couples together."

With all that being said, if you ask the average person, like Lisa, what her core values are, you get this awkward pause, and then the guessing game starts. If you're dating and looking to start a healthy relationship, then identifying your core values might just be a good place to start.

Now that we've discussed core values, let's talk about deal-breakers. Before you think to yourself, "I've already heard about deal-breakers, and I know what mine are. I know exactly what I'm not putting up with," let me say, "Blah, blah, blah, blah and blah!" In my experience, people love to rattle off their deal-breakers until they develop strong feelings for someone.

I can't tell you how many times I've seen people jump into relationships with guys or girls who had four out of five of their deal-breaking behaviors or traits. Why? Because emotions, feelings, and sex can be very powerful and can cause you to blind yourself to things you had already decided weren't okay with you. We could get into the science of it and talk about the release of oxytocin, a bonding hormone. We could also discuss the euphoric feelings that dopamine can give you when you have really great chemistry with someone and all of that, but I have a better idea.

Stop.

Sit back and think about your own experiences or those of any of your friends or family. I'm willing to bet that you know someone who ignored some of his or her deal-breakers, all in the name of love, sex, or attention. With that example in mind, it would be wise for us to define what a deal-breaker is before we jump on the emotional rollercoaster.

Troy's definition of deal-breaker: A non-negotiable reason to cut someone off.

Dictionary.com's (2015) definition of deal-breaker: "Any issue or factor that is significant enough to terminate a negotiation."

All right! Now that you and Lisa are familiar with core values and deal-breakers, you're one step closer to choosing the right person to love.

The goal of this chapter isn't to give you more clichéd ideas about dating, it's to help you change your mindset about how you view those clichés. It's one thing to have values, but it's another thing to apply those values to the mate you're potentially choosing. It's one thing to know your deal-breakers, but it's another thing to follow those instincts even in the midst of love and emotions.

This is about being intentional and disciplined, conscious enough to reflect on whether or not you have been choosing wisely, including the person you are currently dating. This is about picking up the mirror and looking in it, not just reading about some concepts so you feel like you're doing the right thing.

If you want to significantly increase your chances of choosing wisely, do me a favor and slow down when you're dating. Let me tell you why.

4 Reasons You Should Stop Moving So Fast When Dating

I know your hormones are going 150 miles per hour, your heart is pumping 100 beats per minute, and your mind is thinking about that person every second, but allow me to be your yield sign and tell you to slow down.

Sometimes when we're dating, we let our hormones drive the car that our minds should be driving. As a result, we move way too fast. Moving too fast can cause us to end up in unhealthy relationships with weak foundations.

Here are four reasons you should slow down.

1) You've only met the representative.

When we first meet someone, we bring our A game. The A game shows the person who's always dressed to impress, positive, funny, and likable. This person is here to wow you, but she can't and won't stay forever. If you have some patience and slow down, you will soon meet the real person.

Allow people to reveal themselves by being in different situations with them before getting too serious. This is the purpose of the dating phase. You need to know if you can handle their B, C, and D games as well. Don't be left saying, "She was a totally different person. What changed?" The person didn't change. You just didn't take time to get to know the real person in the first place.

2) Sex confuses things and limits your ability to discern.

"But the sex was amazing!"

How many times have you heard someone use this as a reason for staying in a bad relationship? Probably more than you care to count. Many times the connection built through sex blinds us and makes it easy for us to ignore red flags.

It takes more than sex to build a healthy relationship, but sometimes what feels good now can make you overlook what won't be good for you later. Don't let good sex be mistaken for a good relationship match. Slow down because the person who really wants you won't mind waiting for intimacy.

3) The two of you may have different intentions.

She wanted a relationship, but he just wanted to keep it casual. Sound familiar?

When you move too fast, you don't take the time to communicate what your intentions are. Then the awkward and dreadful "What are we?" conversation has to happen. This can be avoided if you slow down and let all intentions be known.

4) Your values may not align.

Your values should be validated by your behavior. Just because the representative you meet in the beginning says she has certain values doesn't mean she lives that way. The only way to know this is to pay attention to consistent actions. It's hard to see consistent, real-life actions when your lips are always locked up and you spend more time bumping and grinding than observing and learning about each other.

Values can make or break a relationship, so pay attention not just to what someone says, but also to what that person does. Please slow down! Patience is key when you're dating. So instead of acting like two impulsive teenagers, take it slow and really get to know what and who you are getting into.

REALITY CHECK FOR LADIES

I can hear the voices of the ladies reading this book right now.

"Okay, Troy, I get it. Love shouldn't hurt. I need to slow down when I'm dating, and I need to choose wisely. I know my values and deal-breakers and all of that. However, I can't seem to meet anyone, and dating has become so difficult. I know you're going to 'teach me how to love,' but I need to find someone to love first, and there aren't any good men out there who are serious about commitment."

Trust me. I hear you. I know you've heard it's a numbers game and that because there are so many more single women than single men, you don't have a chance. They told you that men are more interested in being with foreign women than checking for you. They told you men are weak now, and strong, independent women intimidate them. They told you a lot of things, all of which have managed to make you have a negative mindset about men and dating in general.

Many of you have even given up hope. The vibrant, positive, and feminine woman you used to be has turned into a cold, negative, and skeptical conspiracy theorist who thinks good men don't exist or that a man's number one goal in life is to hurt you.

Stop it. Stop it now, and in fact, if any of your friends have adopted the same mindset, I suggest you break up with them as well...or tell them to read this book!

When it comes to dating, relationships, and love, your mindset can make or break you. What you believe will subconsciously direct your behavior, and your behavior will determine your outcome. The truth of the matter is many times you say you're ready to be in a relationship or marriage, but you aren't truly ready to love. You aren't really ready to rid yourself of the negative experiences your ex put you through, and you aren't ready to open yourself up to the possibility of love. You're in love with the idea of love.

This is the reason you look for the bad in every man you date. This is why you always find an excuse to never go out or leave the house. This is why you refuse to do online dating or to be set up with anyone. This is why, when you do go out, you don't make yourself approachable, you keep your head in your phone, and you avoid eye contact with the cute guy who has been checking you out all night.

This is why you'd rather have man-bashing sessions over red wine with your girls than go out with the man who asked you to dinner months ago. While I understand this doesn't describe all women, I know for a fact someone reading this book just saw herself in the reflection of the mirror that is this page.

Women ask, "Where are all the good men?" I respond, "They are everywhere."

I don't know about you, but everywhere I go, I see men and I see women. The question you have to ask yourself is do you see them too, or have you allowed your past and the negativity of the world to blur your vision?

Has it caused you to miss out on the possibility of love because you're more worried about the possibility of hurt or rejection?

"But I thought this book was about teaching me how to love?!" you say.

How can anyone teach you how to love if you keep telling yourself love doesn't exist?

I'm reminded of another client—let's just call her Monica—who came to me with this negative mindset about men. She could give me every excuse in the world as to why good men weren't finding her. Everything she ever posted on social media had the "Men ain't ish" undertone. She wasn't open to changing anything about herself or her behavior because, of course, she was perfect and any man would be lucky to have her.

According to her, she intimidated all the men in the world. Monica smelled of arrogance, which I later found out was just the scent she was using to cover up her insecurity. Finally I asked her, "If you were a guy, what about would make you want to be with you?" After an awkward pause, she reverted back to listing her accomplishments, but I stopped her and asked the original question, this time in reference to her attitude and mindset. This is where her growth began.

Slowly but surely, her mindset changed, the negative posts turned a little more positive, and she became open to dating again, online and offline. She smiled more, and the feminine side began to ooze out of her again. Men approached Monica more, and she went on numerous dates, some good and some bad.

Then she met him, the guy who was perfect for her. One year later, they were engaged, and she called me on that day to say thank you. I asked, "Well, what are you thanking me for?" Monica replied, "Thank you for the reality check!"

If you really want to know how to love someone, love yourself enough to be honest and do some self-reflection. With reflection comes growth, and with that growth you become more open because you operate from a place of being excited about love instead of insecure about rejection.

Speaking of reality checks, let me share my thoughts about the "strong, independent women" who think the only reason they aren't in a relationship is because they intimidate men.

4 Reasons Why Independent Women Aren't Lonely but Bitter and Unapproachable Ones Are

"Men are just intimidated by me! Why should I have to apologize for my success?"

Those are the cries of the infamous "independent woman" who claims the reason she's single or her relationships don't work is because she's successful. After continuously hearing these statements, I had to do some further investigation from the male perspective. Please realize that even if you, as a woman, don't think this is right, this is how things are being perceived from a male's point of view.

I see you! Stop rolling your eyes and read on, you might just learn something! These are four consistent findings of my research into the difference between truly independent women and bitter, unapproachable women. Are you ready?

1) Bitter or unapproachable women can't turn it off.

CEO, Director, VP, they're all very attractive titles, but when you are dating or in a relationship, men desire a woman, not a boss. Giving orders and making men feel like they're just a notation in your appointment book isn't flattering. It's a turnoff.

Your man is not your subordinate or your child, thus you should act like his mate, not like his mama. Telling him what to do, when to do it, and how to do it doesn't go over well with grown and secure men. Secure men love independent women; in fact, many men find it very sexy. Sometimes it's not that he is intimidated by your title; it's just that he is tired of being treated like your employee.

2) Bitter or unapproachable women are mean.

From what I hear and see, many women will dress up in their best outfit, full makeup, and nicest heels just to go out and look like they don't want to be bothered. They project closed body language and a scowl that screams, "Don't even THINK about talking to me!"

When a regular man (not Shemar Moore, Idris Elba, or Morris Chestnut) gets enough courage to approach them, because he isn't six foot five with bulging muscles, he's met with an attitude that says, "I am so out your league!" For many men, it's not the idea of being turned down; it's the way in which it's done. Even if you aren't interested, it's okay to still be nice.

3) Bitter or unapproachable women have outrageous standards.

Ladies, real men who are secure applaud your success, but the fact of the matter is you don't have to share the same income to share the same values. You making six figures is great, but him making half of that doesn't mean he has less ambition. He may be equally as successful, just not monetarily. By no means am I suggesting you lower your standards, but I am saying base your standards on character and values, not on material things and income.

4) Bitter or unapproachable women believe independent equals entitled.

Okay, I get it. Men are supposed to pursue and court women, but court should not mean chase. Men understand that you don't really "need" a man because you are independent, but that doesn't mean we don't want our efforts to be reciprocated.

Dating and relationships are about reciprocation. Just because you are independent or self-sufficient doesn't mean you are entitled to a man chasing you. Ladies, you are definitely the prize, and men say they don't mind earning that prize, but just because you don't need a man doesn't mean you can't show him you do want him.

Before you totally discredit all of this and close this book with your eyes rolling because you feel attacked, consider this: No matter how independent we are as individuals, we still need each other.

Sometimes it's not about your reality; it's about the perception. As men and women, we can blame each other, or we can seek to understand each other. The choice is yours.

Now before I end this chapter, ladies, please understand I know that some of you don't have any trouble meeting men. In fact, many times you meet a guy and you think everything is great, but ultimately he doesn't choose you. Here is just a little bit of insight on why he may not have chosen you. Sometimes it's you, and sometimes it's him.

4 Reasons He Didn't Choose You

Women often come to me wondering, "Why wasn't I good enough? Why did he choose her and not me?" Funny thing is this question usually comes after she has been engaging in a "friends with benefits situation" or a "no strings attached" type of relationship. I find it interesting that so many people willingly participate in these kinds of exchanges, and then come out of them so scarred. The reason this keeps happening is because oftentimes you engage in these agreements under false pretenses. You go into it saying all you want is something casual, yet when it doesn't graduate into anything serious, you end up hurt, angry, and bitter. Here are a few reasons he didn't choose you.

1) He didn't have to invest anything.

We always hear that people value things more when they earn them, and the same thing holds true in dating and relationships. For some reason, many people started requiring less from relationships and then expecting more. If a man doesn't have to invest any time, energy, resources, or emotion in you the odds of him valuing you enough to make you his wife, or even his girlfriend, are slim to none.

Instead of him having to invest in you so you'll reciprocate, you gave yourself away. You disguised it as you being horny, but in reality the only thing you were horny for was the idea that he might really want to spend time with you. The idea sounds great, until the sex is over and he finds a reason to have to get up and go. Hurts, doesn't it?

2) You tried to change the rules.

You got into this situation claiming to be okay with just having sex. You claimed you wouldn't catch feelings and could handle "no strings attached," but suddenly you started to want to cuddle more, you wanted to kiss more, you wanted more of his time, and finally, you wanted him to take you out in public and show you off.

The problem is that he never planned to do any of those things with you, but you convinced yourself if you sexed him good enough he would. Wrong! You weren't honest about what you truly wanted, even when he was. He didn't lie; he never planned on choosing you. Hurts, doesn't it?

3) He liked her beyond the sex.

Ladies, as shallow as you think men are—I've told you once and I'll tell you again—you have to have substance beyond sex. Most men of substance don't choose wives based on how great sex is with her.

Men who want to build families look for women who can help them accomplish that. I don't care how great your selfies look, how great your sex game is, or how many degrees you have. Nothing can ever replace the nurturing spirit, supportive nature, and the feminine allure of a good woman.

Have you ever noticed that many men don't tend to necessarily marry the best-looking women they can find? They marry the ones they can see themselves building a family and life with. It's the reason why you will sometimes look at what you call a "fine man" with what you might call an "average woman." I bet that average woman had some substance, while you were throwing it back and posting half-naked pictures on Instagram. One day, he decided he needed more than looks alone. Hurts, doesn't it?

4) He wasn't ready yet.

Unfortunately, sometimes you really are a great woman—the complete and total package, but he's too immature to realize that. He isn't in a mature enough season for him to understand what he has right in front of him.

You couldn't understand why he wouldn't just act right, but he was so selfish at that point in his life that he ended up losing out on a good woman. This man usually comes back years later and apologizes for how he treated you, trying to get a second chance. Sometimes him not choosing you has nothing to do with you and everything to do with him. Unfortunately, he had to lose in order to win. Still hurts though, doesn't it?

Teach Me How to Love: Why What You Don't Know Will Hurt You!

These reasons may rub some people the wrong way and may even make some folks get defensive, but at the core of it is pure honesty. You must begin to be honest with yourself about what you want and the situations you put yourself in. The longer you blame, the more you will continue to get hurt.

A NEW LESSON FOR LADIES

Okay ladies, now that you've held the mirror up to your face and realized maybe you aren't as perfect as you thought; let's change the narrative a little. One of the big things I want to accomplish in this book is to help men and women understand a little more about each other, so we can love each other better.

Many times the lessons you're taught about love are very one-sided. Thus, you tend to believe your way is the only way of thinking and that can be toxic for any relationship. The truth of the matter is even if you are a beautiful woman with your own car, own house, own everything, smart as a whip and you know how to cook and clean, those things don't automatically qualify you as a good mate.

Yes, yes, or as the ladies say it now, yasssssss! The things you consider lovable about you don't necessarily certify you to be able to love. I know they told you all you have to do is be the prototype of a wife in order to become one, but have you ever stopped to think less about what you need in love and more about what a man needs in order to be and feel loved?

Do you have it stuck in your mind that men and women need the same things in love? Do you ever find yourself frustrated because you can't understand why men just don't get it? In every failed relationship you've had was the reason it didn't work always because of something he did and never because of anything you did?

A good woman learns how to love her mate the way he needs to be loved, and not the way she wants to love him. With that said, understand that men and women are different and you may have to unlearn some things in order to love a man better.

The women who embrace the principles below see improvements in their relationships, but the women who fight them won't fare as well. The difference between these groups of women is a difference of mindset. One mindset says, "How can I love him better?" While the other mindset says, "Well, what about him and what he doesn't do?" I'll let you guess which mindset is more productive. Check it out.

6 Things Women May Have to Learn in Order to Love Their Men Better

Women are now being taught how to be unstoppable, independent masters of their own lives and careers. Many are forced into doing it all on their own or they've been raised by someone who was forced to do the same. In the midst of all of this greatness, which I applaud, sometimes the one thing that gets lost is how to love a man. Here are a few things that women can do to love their men better.

1) **Allow him to be vulnerable.**

Many times women plead with men to be more emotional and to talk about their feelings, but what I find is many times it's just the woman wanting him to reassure her of how he feels about her. Any other time he begins to express his emotions it's viewed as him being sensitive or needy.

A big part of loving him better is respecting the fact that he has emotions and needs them to be taken seriously. Men don't have many emotional outlets, and when he needs to let his feelings flow or have them acknowledged, he should be able to do that freely with his wife or significant other.

2) Be encouraging and show appreciation.

A huge contributor to loving your man is affirming and appreciating him. As tough as we act as men, there is nothing that keeps us going more than pleasing and being affirmed by our wives.

Just because he is supposed to provide and protect doesn't mean he doesn't love to hear you say that you appreciate it. Just because he is a man, that doesn't mean he doesn't want to hear he's handsome, you're attracted to him, and he rocks your world sexually. Not only does this make him feel loved, but as a result, he will be encouraged to do more to make you happy.

3) Make him want to come home.

A man's house should be his place of peace, not chaos; a place of love, not war. He should be welcomed home with open arms, not with a list of demands and a book full of arguments. Instead of meeting him at the door with all the things he hasn't done around the house, meet him at the door with a smile, a hug, and a kiss that will make him want to rush to get there daily.

Loving your man has a lot to do with the environment you create at home. A house full of peace and love is a house most men love to come home to. If you wonder why he makes three detours before showing up, then you may want to take a look at what he walks into when he arrives.

4) Make him a priority, not an option.

Too often as families are created and kids come into the mix the person left standing to fend for himself is the husband. He's left to fend for himself emotionally, mentally, and sometimes sexually.

One of the best ways to make your husband feel loved is to make him feel like a priority and not an afterthought. That may mean sometimes telling your friends you can't talk on the phone tonight or putting the kids to sleep early. You are making it a point to spend time with the most important person in your life, your husband.

5) Show interest in the things he likes.

I get it. You don't like football, you hate fishing, and you don't know anything about his job, but loving him better means being in tune with him, even when the subject matter doesn't interest you much.

Ladies, your man does not expect you to understand everything about football or know his job as well as you know your own; he just appreciates it when you take an interest. Sometimes he just wants his main lady to sit on the couch with him, cuddle up and watch the game. You don't even have to say a word, because sometimes he just wants you there so he can feel close to you.

6) Don't forget about sex!

I know sometimes you think your man is just a horn dog and all he cares about is sex, however please hear me out: if you want to love him better, you must create a welcoming sexual environment. The environment can't wreak of obligation or always be only on your terms. Sex with you is how he stays connected to you, and satisfying you is how he remains confident in who he is as your husband.

Sometimes the little things about love matter the most, but unfortunately those little things aren't generally taught. I'm sure your man will be happy if you embrace these six things and you might just be happier too.

REALITY CHECK FOR MEN

I see the fellas right now clapping their hands and popping their collars after reading the previous two chapters, but fellas we can't walk around like we're perfect when it comes to this love, dating, and relationship thing. There are some things that we seriously have to unlearn if we want to get this love thing right. They sold us some lies and myths, and it's time that we return them.

We've been sold the lie that conquering women, viewing them as objects, and impressing them with our sexual prowess is the ultimate goal and the cornerstone of our identities. We've been sold the myth that manipulating and controlling women is a sign of strength. We've been sold the lie that our size and strength somehow make us superior to women, even though they are the ones who gave birth to us—so how's that work?

We've been sold a lot of things from society and the media, but it's time to read the fine print. I believe the most powerful thing in the world is a man who knows how to love. When I say love, I mean love himself, his children, others, and most importantly his woman.

You see, although we've been taught the lie that love makes us weak, the truth is it's where our innermost strength lies. We walk around with our chests poked out, with this tough guy stature, yet the things many of us seem to be most afraid of being vulnerable, loving someone else, and allowing ourselves to be loved back.

Instead of getting into the depths that come with building a real bond with someone, we stay on the surface, swimming in the shallow waters of sex and lust. Men, if you've never gotten it before, here is your permission slip making it okay to want to be loved and to give love!

If we are being completely honest with ourselves, ninety percent of us have had a great girl or woman who we knew was perfect for us, but we allowed our inability to love and commit fully to drive her away. She gave us her everything and forgave us time after time for not loving her right. Instead of getting our act together we took advantage of her willingness to stand by us, until one day she had enough and decided to walk away.

If we are being honest with ourselves, most of us realize we were emotionally and physically immature. Trying so hard to keep up with our boys and poke sex partner notches in our belts that we subconsciously started redefining intimacy as nothing more than sex. We would show up to her house and put in A+ performances in the bedroom, only to realize, once the adrenaline stopped flowing and the orgasm was complete, there was nothing there to stop us from wanting to put on our clothes and leave. While she lay in the midst of what she thought was a connection, we knew in our hearts it was really just a booty call.

As we became men, we spent so much time learning how to sex that we never really learned how to love. That becomes evident more than ever when we get tired of just the sex and start looking for the substance, only to find ourselves lost. I was once at the point as well, and as you can expect, I wrote about it in a piece that took my website *XklusiveThoughts.com* to the next level.

I Say Yes! Why I Decided to Get Married!

Okay, so check it out. I'm a little less than a month away from my wedding, and it's finally dawning on me that I am about to be married.

I can see it now. All the ladies reading this are like, "Awwwwwww!" And all the fellas are like, "Are you sure you want to do that?" Surprisingly enough, my answer to that question is yes. Let me explain.

As men, society tells us we are not supposed to be excited about marriage, right? I know we are supposed to be victims of our own sexual appetites, which we lustfully desire to feed with a plethora of women, but ultimately, we are left still hungry for this little thing called substance.

As a result, men fight this internal battle of Sex vs. Substance. While we are busy fighting, we usually end up losing the substance we wanted, while searching for the sex, just to look back and say, "Damn! I lost a good one." How many times have I seen or heard this scenario? I'm choosing the substance over the sex, so I say yes!

With saying yes to the substance, there comes a responsibility. The responsibility is the one that says I will embark on a journey that is bigger than me and my own selfish desires so I may lay a foundation that will build a legacy. You see, as men, we must come to a point where we realize that our legacies are built not by the number of women we conquer, but by the impact we have on our families and the people around us.

How many men are now fifty years old, looking back and regretting the fact that they never did right by their family or never had an impact for which they will be remembered? Too late, they are trying to make up for lost time. I don't want to build my legacy reactively; instead I want to build it proactively, so I say yes!

Another reality that many men won't admit to is that, just as women desire stability and security, men do too. This whole image of a "ride or die chick," Bonnie and Clyde, and all that Hollywood stuff is just a cool way of saying I want and need someone to be here for me when times get tough.

I need someone to share the sunny days and the rain with me. I need someone to encourage me, support me, and believe in me, even when I don't believe in myself. I need someone I can count on to represent me and our family the right way. I need someone to pick me up when I fall. Ultimately, we all just need someone who's going to have our back, so I say yes!

Earlier I mentioned the battle of Sex vs. Substance, and it brings me back to a conversation I had with an old head, during which he said, "You have to think beyond the sex." Being a male, one of the hardest things to do is think beyond the sex. We desire women from a young age, we learn to embrace the chase, and our identities become rooted in sexual conquests.

As a result of the time and energy we invest in validating our manhood through sex, many of us never learn how to validate our manhood through character and family. Now, don't get me wrong. We will always be physically attracted to other women—just as women will be attracted to other men— but it is only after we have learned to think beyond the sex that those thoughts no longer manifest into actions. One thing every guy knows is that if there is no substance behind the sex, then after the orgasm there is no more desire to really even be in her presence. I know every lady believes he wants to stay around and cuddle, but the reality is that no substance = no cuddle = be gone! #TruStory

Every time I tell someone I'm engaged, inevitably, I hear the same things:

"You sure you want to do that?"

"You're too young."

"Why would you give up the single life?"

Being that I am only human, I can't lie and say constantly hearing those things didn't make some sort of impact on my thought process.

Some days, I can't help but wonder, what if, or is it the right decision, or would the streets be more fun? I think this is where the gift of God gave me a vision, which was influenced by the experiences He has put me through in my life. In turn, these experiences have aided in my growth. All of this helped me to value this idea of life being about something bigger than you.

Okay, let me break that down. God put me through some things that forced me to grow up and helped me to see, even early in life, you can work towards fulfilling His vision of you, deciding to be selfless and choosing to do things that are bigger than yourself.

I don't want to get too philosophical, and I won't sit here and act like it's always just that easy. What I will say is that what makes saying yes so easy for me is very simple. It's the fact God put someone in my life with so much substance, who's so genuine and so loving, who's so selfless and not to mention beautiful. She brings out everything good in me, while accepting the bad in me, all while believing in the great in me that has yet to come. With that being said, I say yes!

You may be asking, "Troy, what's the point? What's the message?"

My point is this: Choose substance over sex, and that will allow you to embrace the responsibility of being bigger than yourself. Then you may begin to build your legacy now, instead of trying to rebuild it later, when it's too late. When you do decide to say yes, do it with someone who makes it easy to do so!

I often get asked the question, "When is a man ready to get married?" You can find the answer to those questions and many more by going to visit *XklusiveThoughts.com* and subscribing to my email list. You will be sent a free copy of my first e-book, Teach Me How to Love: A Man's Journey Toward and Through Marriage.

A NEW LESSON FOR MEN

Men, the very first thing we have to do—if we want to have more fulfilled and happier relationships—is to learn that men and women have different needs. This all starts with changing your mindset. You can't expect your woman to be happy with you loving her the same way you ask her to love you. While you may think something is simple, it may be a little more complex when you're dealing with a woman.

In the same way you want her to be different, softer, more nurturing, and more supportive, she needs those very same things from you, but they may come in different packages. She needs more than good food, appreciation, sex, and peace of mind, and the faster we learn this, the more equipped we will be to meet those needs.

As men, we all think we're experts on women because we've been so successful at getting them or having sex with them. However, in reality many of us are lacking in our ability to love and we don't even know it. I know this because while you sit around the house thinking you're the big man on campus and "holding it down," your girlfriend or wife is in my inbox. She's becoming my client so she can try to figure out how to get you to love her better.

So before you get cocky and skip over what I'm trying to tell you, take the time to do some self-reflection. Ask yourself if you're loving her the way you want to love her or the way *she* wants you to love her? Your woman may have different needs than what I write about, but remember, I told you this book isn't a "how to" book; it's a "change your mindset" book.

All I want you to do is be conscious of the fact that you may need to check in and make sure you are fulfilling her physical, mental, and emotional needs. While you may think you're operating at 100% capacity, trust me when I say you may really be at only 25% in her eyes.

Men always say women are emotional, but sometimes we don't take the time to understand what her emotional needs are. Before we go any further, let's define what an emotional need is. According to Mosby's Medical Dictionary (2009) an emotional need is: *"A psychological or mental requirement of intrapsychic origin that usually centers on such basic feelings as love, fear, anger, sorrow, anxiety, frustration, and depression and involves the understanding, empathy, and support of one person for another."*

This all became so clear to me when I was coaching a couple via Skype and we shared an epiphany moment. Now, just to give you context, the only reason the man was in the coaching session was because his woman pretty much twisted his arm and dragged him there. His pride just wouldn't allow him to have another man speak to him about his relationship. I felt the tension for the first thirty minutes, and then I had him do an exercise. I asked him to tell me the top four emotional needs his woman had in the relationship. Mind you, she'd already told me her top four, which were:

1) Security
2) Admiration
3) Appreciation
4) Being supported

This is what his list was:
1) Security
2) Respect
3) Value
4) Being understood

Now, if you take a look at those lists, there is only one thing they have in common, and that's a need for security.

As the coaching session continued, what I found was the emotional needs he listed weren't truly her needs, but were more of his own needs. **This just in:** Here lies the problem in many relationships, but it's an easy fix if we communicate early and often and when men learn some new behaviors.

5 Behaviors Men May Have to Learn to Love Their Women Better

I thought about the many wives and girlfriends who are my clients and whose chief complaint is that their husbands or boyfriends don't show they care enough or aren't affectionate enough.

While I understand as men we tend to express love by what we do rather than what we say, there are some ways we can meet the emotional needs of our mates by doing a few things differently. These are things we aren't necessarily taught and without them being modeled for us, how do we learn them? Ask yourself these questions and apply the tips.

Are you the man who only tells her you love her when you are making up for something wrong?

1) Make telling her you love her a habit.

For many men, mentioning the "L" word automatically puts you in a position of weakness, but I'm here to tell you that she needs to hear it. She doesn't just need to hear it when you are trying to make up for a wrongdoing, but she needs to hear it just because you woke up next to her. What you may feel is mushy or soft makes her feel like your relationship is secure and strong. Make it a habit to tell her you love her.

Are you the man who tries to fix all of her problems before you actually listen to them?

2) Listen to her. No, really listen to her.

Confession: I'm guilty of not listening as well. As men, we are so solution-oriented that we sometimes won't even let her finish her sentence before we are trying to figure out how to fix her problem. Sometimes, she just needs you to listen, and what you will find is when you really listen, she'll come up with her own solution. She leaves that conversation feeling loved, not because you gave her a solution, but because you listened to her problem.

Are you the man who only kisses her when you are trying to have sex?

3) Kiss her and touch her "just because."

The power of touch is essential in a relationship. Take that extra second to kiss her before you leave, or kiss her while she's still asleep. It's a small part of intimacy that keeps you connected, and it helps her to feel loved and reassured.

Hold her hand while you're out in public; it means more to her than you know. Sometimes as we get settled in a relationship, we forget that showing affection is what keeps us connected.

Are you the man who only fits her into your schedule after you're done with your work?

4) Make her a priority.

Yes, I've been guilty of this one as well, but now that I'm conscious of it, I've made changes. As men we feel like our duty is to provide so we can put our jobs and careers before our mate. We only make time for her in between time, when sometimes she just wants you to choose her first.

Choose her first. I'm not saying you have to do this every day, but making her a priority makes her feel loved, and when she feels loved, she will make sure you have everything you need to keep being great in your career.

Are you the guy who never notices anything different about your mate until she points it out?

5) Notice her.

Men, our women are always doing things to try and get our attention, and it's up to us to notice. When she changes her hair, buys a new outfit, or puts on a different fragrance, it's imperative you don't just think it looks or smells good. It's important to her that you acknowledge it. A big part of loving your woman is being in tune with her, and this shows you are in tune. Besides she's probably doing it for you anyway.

Most men are taught how to be strong and tough, but we aren't taught that some of our strength lies in our ability to be soft and in our ability to love. Men understand it's okay not to know how to love, but it's not okay to remain ignorant. Seek help, advice, and resources to help you improve your ability to love.

SECURITY

In the last chapter I asked the couple to identify the woman's top emotional needs, and the number one need was security. Merriam-Webster (2014) defines secure as: "Protected from danger or harm." I believe there's more to that story and we must start thinking about security in a different way. Men must start looking differently at how they make a woman feel secure, and women must start looking differently at what they view as security.

According to psychologist Abraham Maslow's "hierarchy of needs," the second most foundational requirement for humans is safety and security. This means that many of our life decisions come from this place of needing to feel secure, and this includes deciding which mate to choose. However, one issue that I see is many women will let this fundamental need drive them to remain in unhealthy relationships. Another issue is that men will falsely think they make a woman feel secure, when really they're just intimidating.

Let me give you an example. If you're a woman reading this book, have you ever stayed in a relationship way too long because you feared being alone? In your eyes does being alone put you in a less secure situation? Maybe that means you won't have that joint income anymore, or maybe that means there won't be anyone around to protect you from intruders or even to secure your future with.

If you're a man reading this book, maybe you think making her feel secure means if another man tries to approach her, you will check him. If you're walking on the sidewalk, you walk on the outside in case a car runs off the road. Maybe you think it means being domineering or controlling.

The key to forming next-level healthy and happy relationships lies in our ability to be completely vulnerable. Vulnerability needs a secure environment in order for it to thrive, and it can be toxic and unhealthy when someone has a false sense of security with a mate.

A lack of real security can cause you to fear being alone and can even cause you to make bad choices in a mate. On the flip side, a real sense of security can bring the best out of a man or woman. It will make you feel comfortable being vulnerable with your fears, feelings, desires, wants, and needs. In other words, security allows us to get real with one another.

If you want to get the most out of your mate, you have to be willing to go all in. One of the reasons we have so much surface-level dating is because people are afraid and don't feel as if the other person will protect and secure their heart. So security is key, but it has to be the real security and not some false sense of security. Luckily, there are specific ways a man can help a woman feel secure in their relationship.

<u>10 Ways to Make Your Woman Feel Secure in Your Relationship</u>

"Make her feel secure in your relationship, and she will move mountains for you!"

Teach Me How to Love: Why What You Don't Know Will Hurt You!

The number of "Amen!" and "Preach!" comments I received from women when I posted that statement let me know there must be some serious truth to it.

As I began to think, I realized men might have a slight disconnect between making our woman feel physically secure and making her feel secure in our relationships or marriage. Sometimes, men believe that making our woman feel secure is about being willing to defend her from a guy who disrespects her or being able to shield her from harm.

While jumping in front of cars, rescuing her from a burning building, or getting up at night to see what that noise was does make her feel protected, there are still some things we can do to make her feel secure in the relationship or marriage.

1) Make love to her like it matters.

One of the safest feelings a woman gets is when you are making passionate love to her. The key term there is passionate. She needs to know that it matters to you, that you're not just going through the motions. Passion creates a feeling of security. Just watch how safe she feels when you hold her in your arms when you're done.

2) Don't gawk at other women when you're together.

I'm a guy, so I understand that men are visual creatures. But we all know there's a difference between looking at a woman and gawking at a woman. Part of making your woman feel secure comes out of how you respect her in public. Gawking at other women is an easy way to hurt her feelings, and it won't make her feel secure in your relationship. If you react like a teenage boy to an attractive woman when you are with her, she can only imagine what you do when she isn't with you.

3) Invest in your family and your children.

Your family and children are of the utmost importance to your wife, thus the more invested you are in them the more secure she will feel about your relationship. Watching you invest not just your money but your time and energy into the family and children will make your wife smile with her heart. It will also speak to the strength of your relationship because of the team effort.

4) Don't make her compete.

When you asked her to be your woman, she obliged under the assumption she wouldn't be in competition for you with other women anymore. Now, let me preface this by saying we should all continue to do the same things we did in order to get our mates. Falling off is not acceptable, but she doesn't want to feel the pressure from you, always flirting with other women, not knowing what kind of boundaries to establish, etc. Failing to protect your relationship from the advances of other women won't make her feel secure in the relationship. It will make her feel like you always have one foot out the door, making it harder for her to go all in.

5) Show and tell her.

Just like men want to feel appreciated, women do as well. Let her know you appreciate her work, her nurturing, her "domestic goddess" skills, and her mothering. It makes her feel secure when she knows all that she does isn't being taken for granted. Men often just want to show, but sometimes she needs to hear you say it.

6) Be faithful.

Being unfaithful tears down so many of the protective walls of your relationship, but being faithful builds them up and fortifies them. Not allowing other people to disrespect your union and not investing your physical and emotional energy into another lets her know that she can be completely vulnerable to you with her heart, feelings, and sexual well-being. Be dependable and consistent. Be a man of your word. Show up when you say you will, and do what you say you are going to do. It's as simple as that.

7) Be assertive and clear.

Take initiative and make decisions. Women don't typically like or respect indecisive men. Sometimes you need to put a little bass in your voice and make a final decision. Your woman looks to you for leadership and guidance and when you can provide that she knows she can feel secure within the relationship with you—her man!

8) Praise her instead of criticizing her in public.

Praising your woman in public lets her know you appreciate her and aren't afraid to profess it to the world. This puts other people on notice that you are your mate's biggest fan, and it makes her put a little extra oomph in her walk. On the flip side, criticizing her in front of others embarrasses her, and it will cut her down in a way that makes her feel she can't trust you with her flaws, and no woman ever wants to feel that way about her man.

9) Be thoughtful.

Being thoughtful and considerate lets her know you care. This means when the holidays come around you put some effort into making them special for her. Listen to her and do things "just because," so she knows you are engaged and listening. Watch the security points add up!

Men must remember that making a woman feel secure in your relationship spans far beyond putting a ring on it. It takes a consistent effort, but the reward is so worth it. Remember: Make her feel secure in your relationship, and she will move mountains for you!

10) Be dependable and consistent.

Be a man of your word. Show up when you say will and do what you say you are going to do. It's as simple as that.

PSUEDO-RELATIONSHIPS

I interrupt this book for a public service announcement:

Situationships, textationships, friend with benefits, no strings attached, and arrangements are not the same things as a committed relationship. They aren't relationships, and they sure aren't marriages!

Relationships took a wrong turn when people started calling them everything but what they are. Some say it's just semantics; I call it the death of commitment. When we started claiming that titles just confuse things, we started confusing ourselves more than ever. Oh, and please don't be fooled. This isn't just a "young person's" problem; this is a problem going on in every age group.

I'm reminded of a meme. Y'all know the one that reads, "You know she's official when it's unofficial and she's still loyal!" Every time I see that meme my stomach starts to hurt because it's so indicative of what we've started to settle for and what we must change our mindsets about immediately. **This just in:** If you want to truly feel secure and fulfilled, and if you want to begin to build a healthy relationship, then you must get out of the gray area of dating.

Take a second and think back to the days before you found this little thing called an ego and before you began to overanalyze everything. It was as simple as a note that read, "I like you. Do you like me? Check YES or NO!"

Fellas, remember when, if you liked a woman, you would pursue her with everything you had and you would pull out all of the stops? Love letters, flowers, love notes left for her to find... anything for a chance at making her your girlfriend. You know before all of the ego and fear of rejection kicked in.

Ladies, remember when you liked a guy and you couldn't stop thinking about him all day? You blushed every time he walked by, and you would be sure to find a way to cross his path, some way, somehow. You know, before you feared being called desperate or "thirsty." The one thing that is consistent in all of these young love scenarios is clarity.

Let's be honest with ourselves. Most times when someone settles for these pseudo-relationships, it's usually because one person is more invested than the other one. One person wants clarity and wants to build something real, but the fear of loneliness allows him or her to lean on the possibility of the situationship turning into a relationship.

If you ever want to know if this is true, then ask yourself or that person this simple question. If you were given the choice to be in this situation or to be in a committed relationship, which one would you choose?

If you desire true commitment and a healthy relationship, then you must start with having true standards about whom and what you will allow into your life. I remember coaching a client of mine who was in a gray area situation. The sad part is that all of her girlfriends were cosigning the ambiguity of the situation, which left her even more confused.

She informed me that she and the guy had been casually seeing one another, but it wasn't official. They were intimate on a regular basis, and he acted as if he liked her beyond just the sex. He was giving her mixed signals, but the one thing he made clear was that he wasn't ready for a relationship.

That presented a problem because she had fallen for the guy and she wanted something more stable. At this point, I informed her that she had a serious choice to make. At first, she went down the road of trying to blame him for leading her on and being unclear, but I quickly let her know that this was on her! I had to get her to change her mindset about the situation.

I asked her how come it was okay for her to invest her time, resources, emotions, and even body in him, yet she didn't even require a commitment for it? Why was it okay for her to put everything into him when she only got back a piece of him? Why was it okay for her to want a relationship but be willing to settle for nothing more than the idea of one?

This coaching session wasn't about how she could get him to change his mind; it was about why she needed to change hers. When you see yourself as valuable, you become stricter about whom and what you allow in your life. You seek clarity, you become empowered, and you begin to live on *your* terms.

That's the conversation I had with my client, and as a result she had a conversation with the guy she was seeing. She didn't blame him. She merely thought more of herself, enough to remove herself from the ambiguous situation.

The moral of the story is that empowered and valuable people don't take what they get; they go get what they want. If you want success in dating or in your relationships, you must allow your values, morals, and standards to guide you instead of your fear, emotions, and sex drive. If you're still finding yourself in these ambiguous situations, let me share some more insight to help you find your way out.

BooThang or MyThang—Which One Are You?

"We just kickin it!"

"We chillin!"

"That's my boo thang!"

Now how many of you have heard these lines before? What about this one? "We don't need a title because titles just confuse things." I know y'all have heard that one.

I'm sure I'll catch some flak for this from all the people who use these phrases as their cop out, but hey, I always welcome the debate. Is it just me? Am I the only one who believes that titles don't confuse things? If anything, they help to define things.

I'm not talking about a person who just met somebody and they've only been dating for a few weeks. I'm not talking about the "cut buddies" who are happy with their arrangement. I'm addressing the people who have been dealing with someone for months, or even years, but still can't seem to figure out what they are doing with that person.

Look, if you're perfectly fine with the ambiguity of the phrases I used above then hey, if you like it, I love it! The only problem I see with this issue is that people only seem to use these phrases when it's convenient for them. Let me explain.

Teach Me How to Love: Why What You Don't Know Will Hurt You!

How come most people are only boo thangs until the other person wants to see someone else? How come y'all just "kickin it" until he or she don't answer your calls and text messages for a few days? How come y'all "just chillin" until he or she makes somebody else a priority over you or don't have the time to chill with you? Do y'all see where I'm going with this?

The problem is that most people who are doing these things either really believe they can handle it this way or are avoiding commitment because they still want to leave their options open for when it's convenient for them (when they meet someone else), or are afraid to ask for a commitment because of the fear of scaring the other person away (they would rather have something than nothing).

The bottom line: There comes a certain time in adulthood when being a "boo thang" is more of a liability than an asset. Most people desire true companionship, but many people don't want to sacrifice their own selfishness in order to get it. What you must understand is that when a person is all in and truly in love with you, that person will naturally want to be with and around you. Not necessarily in a crazy, stalker way, but in a way that says, "I want your time, your love, your trust, your companionship more than I want the potential to find it somewhere else!" In other words, they will commit to you. When it's special and it's real, you will move from "boo thang" to "my thang" because the open door that is associated with keeping you as a boo thang is no longer worth it, and they will close it!

So what's my point?

My point is that many of you are settling for being a boo thang and investing your time, effort, and emotional energy in something that you can't define now and probably won't be able to define in the future.

If you think you can accept that role and eventually it will just happen, then you need to wake up. If a person has no fear of losing you, then you accept the role of being a boo thang. You better believe you will remain just that; that's until they find someone else they can't risk losing, and who won't accept it.

I'm not saying you should run around giving ultimatums or anything like that. What I am saying is that sometimes we get so comfortable with a situation that we never step back and reevaluate it. Sometimes we are so scared of losing something we accept, even if we know it's ultimately not what we really want.

Why settle for being a boothang when you can be a mythang? Remember titles don't confuse things; titles define things. I would argue the title of boo thang is one that is usually not desired; it's one that is tolerated.

DATING "POTENTIAL"

Your intuition told you it wasn't a good idea, but your hormones made you feel like you could change her. You knew it was a risk taking a chance on his potential but at the time, that was a risk you were willing to take. It was better than being alone.

It was easier to believe in the dream because facing the reality meant you might have to make a choice between Saturday nights alone in a cold bed and Saturday nights with a warm body next to you. There were so many red flags all covered up by what you thought was potential.

This is an issue I see so many people struggle with because most of us want to see people more for who they could be, rather than for who they really are. We've all been there before, but it's time that we get real with ourselves and with others.

If you really want to find someone you can build a healthy and long-lasting relationship with, then base it on shared values. Don't base it on the hope that the person will magically turn into who you want or need. Shared values won't guarantee the relationship will work out, but it will at least give it the best chance by helping you to establish a strong foundation.

If you like succinct lists, here are five reasons that you should not date a person based mostly on potential.

5 Reasons You Shouldn't Date Someone Who "Has Potential"

1) The potential may never come to fruition.

Everybody is born with the potential to do a lot of things, but not everyone will end up doing those things. I might have the potential to be a millionaire, but if I'm not putting any work towards making that happen, then you can't trust that it will. This is why you must let your values— instead of your hormones or fear of loneliness—drive your decision-making when you choose a mate.

2) You don't have the power to change anyone.

No matter how great you think you are, you still don't have the power to make someone change because change is an inside job. Your great career, nurturing spirit, great cooking, or good sex won't get the job done.

3) You will end up resentful and bitter towards the person.

What happens after all of the lust is gone and the chemistry dies down? If that person doesn't turn out to be the partner you dreamed of you get angry with him or her.

This happens a lot when a woman meets a man who has no job, no money, and no ambition, but she sees that he has potential. That's until six months later when he's still lying on the couch playing PlayStation and eating cereal while she is at work all day. Suddenly she grows angry and resentful, and eventually, the relationship becomes dysfunctional—all in the name of potential.

4) You are ready now!

If you've taken the time to develop yourself to be ready to date and get into a real and healthy relationship, if a possible love interest comes your way and says he or she isn't ready for a relationship or even looking for one, believe it, and run in the other direction.

If you are ready to seriously date with the goal of getting into a committed relationship, no matter how awesome this guy or gal might be, you must be willing to remove yourself because your intentions don't align. He or she may ooze potential, but the intentions don't match yours.

5) You're too old for that.

There comes a point in life when your track record needs to be established and your actions and behaviors must align with your words. You shouldn't be thirty-five trying to help a potential mate realize his or her potential. At that point the person should have something established, and if he or she should be working on themselves in order to do so. You don't have time to be someone's parent when you want to be his or her lover!

The bottom line is people don't have to be perfect for you to date them, but your values need to align and their behaviors need to reflect those values. If words and actions don't align, then potential won't bridge the gap! Choose wisely my friends.

WHEN IT'S RIGHT, IT'S EASY

Why do we make love and relationships so hard? Why do we let the thing that's supposed to feel so good cause us the most pain and confusion? Sometimes love is so hard because we try to force it out of someone who isn't capable of giving it to us. It's hard because we tend to want to love people not for who they are but for who we want them to be.

We fall in love with potential instead of actions so we end up disappointed when we realize that the person as is won't work out for us long term. We chase people who don't want to be caught and then become exhausted once we realize they really never had any intention to commit to us. As a result we end up actually running away from the people who actually do want to love us. Love becomes hard because we want to withdraw everything without depositing anything. We end up wanting everyone to prove themselves to us instead of proving ourselves to each other. Finally we get burned out on love because we focus on the feelings more than the actions not realizing that love, when done right, requires action.

I often say, "When it's right, it's easy," and I stand by that statement. When you look at people who are in happy and healthy relationships, you don't hear many stories about the games that were played or any trickery involved to get in the relationship. There probably was never a need to have a "what are we?" conversation or to give any ultimatums.

Additionally, when you see people in happy, healthy relationships, they might admit that while it takes effort, they don't mind putting it in because it's worth it. When someone is truly into you and wants to be with you it will be obvious.

I've seen so many clients trying to force a relationship with the wrong person that they miss out on the right person.

I'm reminded of a client who was infamous for putting all of the right guys in the friend zone, while at the same time trying to convince all of the wrong guys to want to be with her. Let's just call her Amanda (another made up name of course!) You may know someone like Amanda. She is the type of person who usually tries to convince herself that she knows exactly why the guy she's dating doesn't want to commit. She will say things like, "Well, he has been hurt in the past and because of that he is so afraid to be in a relationship, so I'm just helping him work through those issues so that we can be together." She also said things to me like, "I'm just being patient with him because once he gets all of his finances and things in order we will be together."

Time out and flag on the play! That's what I told her when she gave me her own diagnosis of a guy who just told her he wasn't interested in a being in a committed relationship with her. Yes, those were his exact words. It's almost like she wanted to play doctor and help heal his case of commitment phobia as she called it instead of just accepting the fact that they did not want the same thing.

After months of coaching, I helped her identify that her true problem was that she wanted to feel accomplished by changing a man's mind or by helping him transform. She realized that trying to force a relationship with someone who doesn't want it was stopping her from entertaining the men who actually saw the value in her and were ready for commitment. Three months later, Amanda had begun dating a great guy with shared values and when I checked in with her she said, "You were right, coach. When it's right, it's easy!"

Understand this. If you have to force it or justify a relationship, then you probably shouldn't be in it. I once heard Bishop T.D. Jakes say in one of his sermons, "There is no relationship without reciprocation." This means that both people in the relationship or dating scenario should be putting in the same amount of effort. If one calls, the other should call as well. If one person arranges dates and activities, the other person should be willing to do the same things. If one person shows affection, the other person should show affection as well. It should be a push-pull mentality, and it should not feel as if one person is always tiring themselves out by doing things such as initiating all of the contact, planning all of the activities, or using all of their resources, while the other person just sits back and receives. That's not easy; that's exhausting.

If you constantly find yourself in dating situations or relationships in which you aren't receiving any reciprocation, then you need to rethink your dating and relationship strategy. If your dating life is exhausting you because of a lack of reciprocation then you must:

1) **Acknowledge what is not happening, and then communicate what you would like to see change.** Be very specific, as sometimes it truly is just a lack of communication. For example, if you are a caller and he or she is a texter, yet you would like to talk more often, then you must say this specifically. It could sound like this: "You know I really want to continue to get to know you, but the way I really get to know someone is by talking. It would really mean a lot to me if you could call more than you text me and if we could see each other face to face more often."

2) **Look for consistent action and change.** If you make something clear and specific and you don't see consistent change, then odds are the person you're dating really doesn't care to change the behavior.

3) **Be willing to cut your losses.** One of the things we find hardest to do is to cut someone off after we have invested time, energy, effort, and resources in them. Always ask yourself, "How much more should I continue to invest if I know I won't get a return on that investment?"

4) **Learn and move on.** Take the time to reflect so that you don't continue to repeat the same behaviors over, and over, and over again.

When it's right, it's easy—not perfect, but easy!

I CAN'T LET GO

Some of you reading this book are wondering how on earth you're supposed to do anything I advise in this book when you can't seem to let go of your past or your ex. Some of you are still hurting and trying to find healing. Others of you have given up on love because it always seems to end up leaving you in pain.

Maybe you gave someone all of you and you only got half of that person in return and now you're stuck with a heart that's on zero. Maybe it was your parents or a family member who betrayed you, or maybe you're just angry at yourself.

Sometimes you hold on for so long hoping things will change only to be met with disappointment time and time again. I hear you, and I feel your pain. I hope this chapter can help you to begin the healing process so you too can begin to love, or to love again.

The first thing you must understand about healing is that it is an active process. I know you've heard "time heals all wounds," and while that has some truth, just like with anything in life if you want something different you have to do something differently. In this case, you need the 4 A's to healing.

1) ALLOW yourself to feel. If you need to cry, then cry. If you want to be angry, then be angry. Own those feelings and emotions, but don't wallow in them forever.

2) ACCEPT that you probably played a role in the demise of the relationship. Whether you failed to choose wisely, allowed yourself to be mistreated, or you were a bad mate, you must accept responsibility.

3) ACKNOWLEDGE that it's over and it's time to move on. Say it, speak it, and then live it. Once you acknowledge it and stop hoping to revive the relationship, then you can truly begin to move on.

4) ASSUME new passions, plans, and activities. Take some time to do some new things and meet some new people. This will help the healing process by occupying your time and exposing you to new possibilities.

Okay. Now that I've given you some tips on how to heal from past hurts and pains, I want to give you a few tips on how to let go of that ex you just can't seem to get out of your life.

The End of the Road: 3 Steps to Letting Go

I really want you to pay attention to this because it's so important. So many people are in a very miserable place in life because they won't let go of the person that caused the misery in the first place.

Although I could dress this up and put in a lot of colorful words, similes and metaphors, I want to get straight to the point. These are three things I want you to do so that you can begin to let go.

1) Stop communicating with your ex.

Look folks, this halfway breaking up thing does not work. If you're going to claim to be breaking up with someone, then you need to seriously break up, and that starts with stopping the communication.

That means all of the texting, talking, emailing, Twittering, Facebooking, or whatever you're doing to stay connected has to cease. If you have kids together, then I know you must communicate, but it should only be about the kids.

"Well," you ask "why can't we be friends?" Here are a few specific reasons why you should reconsider trying to be friends with your ex.

Proximity will cause issues.

The bottom line is that when a person is an ex and you were truly in love— no matter how y'all broke up—there are still numerous reasons that you were in love with them. Sometimes sheer proximity will not let those feelings go away. So this means that y'all texting, calling, skyping, communicating, and hanging out is nothing but a breeding ground for those feelings to resurface and cause confusion.

I don't care who you are or how rational you are, if you have ever been in love, you know that just saying you're broken up isn't enough. Breaking up is a process. It's a process that's almost never successful as long as the two people are trying to be "friends" and do things the same way they always have, only without the title. Please remember that committing and breaking up are both actions. Just because you use the words doesn't mean you are necessarily practicing the actions!

You will turn off potential new mates!

When you are trying to pursue a new relationship, but you make your ex a priority, the only thing you do is send signs to the new person that he or she isn't as important. When you are always justifying and defending why you and your ex still talk so much, or you act as if it's not that big of a deal, you immediately begin to lose "trust points" with the new person.

Don't act like you've never been dating a girl or guy who is always communicating with an ex, but when you ask why, they say, "Trust me. It's not that big a deal!" What they don't know is that you are thinking, "No, I don't trust you, and furthermore, if it's not that big a deal, then why does it seem like such a priority!" Seriously, how many times do people have to lose out on someone who is good for them because they spend so much time trying to be cool with someone who has proven not to be good for them?

You may set yourself up to be hurt again.

The other thing that people seem not to remember is that your ex will almost always tell you everything you want to hear and all of sudden want to change when he or she feels that you might move on for real. Most of the time "for real" is when you are becoming interested in someone new.

If you think I'm lying, think about that friend who you know keeps sabotaging any new relationships because she runs back to her ex when he all of sudden wants to work things out. Look…I'm not saying that your ex can't change, but I am saying stop ruining your chances at future happiness because you keep focusing on the words of your ex and not the actions of your ex. The person is your ex for a reason!

Sometimes you have to make room for your blessings, and many times that's not possible because you are holding on to what was, instead of focusing on what could be. Communicating with your ex will slow down your healing and "getting over it" process, so just don't do it. Oh and by the way, this includes sex! This whole "we broke up, but we're still going to be friends with benefits" thing must stop. I don't care how horny you get or how good the sex is, you must close your legs so that you can eventually close your heart.

2) Learn from the experience.

If there's one thing I can't have any sympathy for it's a person who continues to make the same mistake over and over and over again. The two of you may have had some great times, but I'm almost willing to bet the bad times are the reason he or she is your ex now. Stop trying to bury the bad things and keep alive the good things just so you can justify playing this double–dutch, back-and-forth game.

We can all learn different things from every experience and relationship, but what you can't continue to do is set yourself up for failure by making the same mistakes over and over.

When you don't learn from your past, you are doomed to repeat it. That's the reason many people would rather stay in their safe and comfortable bad situation: they're afraid of making the same mistake again. Accept the fact that it's over, and embrace the lessons you learned from the situation. If you took an L (loss), then take that L, and better prepare yourself for a W (win) later.

3) **Wave the white flag.**

What I mean is this: stop trying to win the situation. So what if he has a new girl or she has a new man? So what if that new person "don't have nothing" on you? The bottom line is that you are still not allowing yourself to let go of the situation because you're still fighting for a person who's your EX! Ask yourself this: even if you win, what kind of prize are you getting?

You don't have to try and win back your ex to prove a point to yourself. At the end of the day, your ex is the one who's winning because he or she probably has both of y'all. So in this case, even if you think you're winning, you are still losing. Besides, your ultimate win and revenge will be when you let go and move on completely.

The hardest thing to accept is when you figure out your ex really doesn't care anymore and has moved on. When your ex sees you do that, that's when you are really #WINNING!

I can already hear it. I'm listening to the thoughts of the people reading this, people who aren't truly ready to let go, and the first thing they're saying is, "Well, that's easier said than done!"

Teach Me How to Love: Why What You Don't Know Will Hurt You!

Well, isn't everything?! Just because something isn't easy, doesn't mean it doesn't need to be done.

Many of you must let go of what's wrong now so you can hold on to what's right later. There are a million other tips I could give to help people let go, but these three are a great starting point. If you aren't ready to receive these three strategies, then odds are you aren't truly serious about letting go. But when you get serious, you know where to find the information you need.

TIME TO REFLECT—LET'S WORK!

The purpose of this section is for you to take all of the things you've learned and bring them to a practical and applicable level so that you can truly change your mindset.

In the exercises that follow I have shared a takeaway quote from each chapter and after each quote I ask a question for you to reflect on. This is by far the most important part of helping you change your mindset so take the time to really think through your answers. Think of this as a journal of sorts, meant to help you get to the next level in love! If you are reading this electronically, get a dedicated journal or notebook specifically designed for you to work through these questions.

I want us to stay in touch! So that I can consistently give you good content to keep you on track, take a few seconds and visit *XklusiveThoughts.com* and subscribe to my email list.

HAPPILY EVER AFTER

"Maybe your family looked like the Huxtables to the public, but was dysfunctional in private. Maybe you don't even realize what you've known all your life is really unhealthy dating or relationships, and it's become so normal to you that you really believe it's right. I call that "normalized dysfunction."

How do you describe a healthy relationship? What qualities have you seen in relationships that you consider healthy?

BE "THE ONE"

"Don't be so focused on finding the one; instead, focus on being the one!"

What qualities and characteristics do you possess that make you "the one?" What areas in your life could you improve that would make you better prepared to be someone's mate?

IT'S NOT THEM—IT'S YOU

"The truth of the matter is that you have to take time to figure out what role you've played in your own dating struggles and failed relationships."

Think about your past relationship failures. What role did you play in the relationship not working? If you could go back to the past now, what would you do differently?

DON'T BELIEVE THE HYPE

"Oftentimes one of the biggest reasons why relationships fall apart is because we get with the person not for who they are, but for who we hoped they would be."

List your top 5 values (nothing materialistic, only character traits such as honesty, ambition, spirituality, etc.) and list your top 5 deal-breakers (things you have **zero** tolerance for when it comes to a future mate, such as dishonesty, irresponsibility, lack of ambition, etc.). Allow these values and deal-breakers to drive your choice in a mate.

CHOOSE WISELY, MY FRIENDS

It's one thing to have values, but it's another thing to apply those values to the mate you're potentially choosing. It's one thing to know your deal-breakers, but it's another thing to follow those instincts in the midst of love and emotions.

Think about a time in your dating or relationship life when you went against your instincts. Why did you ignore your instincts? What were the results?

REALITY CHECK FOR LADIES

"When it comes to dating, relationships, and love, your mindset can make or break you. What you believe will subconsciously direct your behavior, and your behavior will determine your outcome."

What is usually your mindset when you meet a guy or when you go out on a date? What kinds of thoughts dominate your mind? Are the thoughts positive or negative?

A NEW LESSON FOR LADIES

"Have you ever stopped to think less about what you need in love and more about what a man needs in order to be and feel loved?"

List some of the ways men may need to be loved differently than women. What specific things can you do to make sure your man is being loved the way he needs to be loved?

REALITY CHECK FOR MEN

"If we are being completely honest with ourselves, ninety percent of us have had a great girl or woman who we knew was perfect for us, but we allowed our inability to love and commit fully to drive her away."

Fellas, think of a situation in which you had a great girl or woman but your fears, actions, or behaviors drove her away. If you could travel back in time, what would you do differently?

A NEW LESSON FOR MEN

"The same way you want her to be different, softer, more nurturing, and more supportive, she needs those very same things from you, but they may come in different packages."

List some of the ways women may need to be loved differently than men. What specific things can you do to make sure your woman is being loved the way she needs to be loved?

SECURITY

"Men must remember that making a woman feel secure in your relationship spans far beyond putting a ring on it. It takes a consistent effort, but the reward is so worth it."

What is the "consistent effort" the above sentence speaks of? Have you always put in the right effort to make your woman feel secure in your relationship? If not, where do you think you've fallen short and can improve?

PSEUDO-RELATIONSHIPS

"If you want to truly feel secure and fulfilled, and if you want begin to build a healthy relationship, then you must get out of the gray area of dating."

What does the gray area of dating look like? What can you do to make sure you have more clarity in your dating situations?

DATING "POTENTIAL"

"Your intuition told you it wasn't a good idea, but your hormones made you feel like you could change her. You knew it was a risk taking a chance on his potential but at the time, that was a risk you were willing to take. It was better than being alone."

Have you ever dated someone based on potential? How did that work for you? What have you learned from this chapter that will help you to do things differently?

WHEN IT'S RIGHT IT, IT'S EASY

"We fall in love with potential instead of actions, and we chase people who don't want to be caught. Love becomes hard because we want to withdraw everything without depositing anything. Love seems hard because we focus on the feelings more than the actions."

Have you ever dated someone because of his or her potential? Were there red flags that you ignored? List some of those red flags along with others that you now want to avoid while dating or in a relationship.

I CAN'T LET GO

"So many people are in a very miserable place in life because they won't let go of the person that caused the misery in the first place."

What's making you hold on to someone who isn't good for you? What attracted you to him or her in the first place? What are the important actions you need to implement from this chapter?

THE TAKEAWAY: DEAR YOU

After reading this book, write a letter to yourself. Write about how you've self-reflected on your dating and relationship life, and write about what you plan to do differently. Look in that mirror, forgive yourself, and start creating your new dating or relationship life today!

Dear Old Me,

ACKNOWLEDGMENTS

To the love of my life, my number one supporter, my biggest critic and my biggest fan, and most importantly, my wife and mother of my child, I just want to say thank you, Tiffini Spry, for all you are to me and to our family.

To my twin sister, Joy Spry, you have literally been by my side since birth, and you continue to be there for me every step of the way. Thanks for being my "big little sister." I love you!

To my dad, Keith Spry, thank you for creating me and thanks for the lessons you've taught me over the years. Things haven't always been perfect, but know that I love you.

To my grandmother Edith Spry, thank you for being the most loving and selfless woman I know. You are the rock of our family, and your encouragement from a young age does not go unnoticed. I love you, "Mama Edee!"

To the GAM Squad, my core group of friends who have joined me on this journey of life and who have been my road team, encouragers, and the ones who have always kept me grounded. Emeka Smalls, James "Sweets" Jones, Cedric "CJ" Jackson, Barry "BJ" Thomas, and Micqueal "Queal" Thompson, I love y'all like my brothers. Thank you!

To my frat brothers from the Lamda Gamma Chapter of Kappa Alpha Psi, thanks for all of the support and thanks for the brotherhood. Special shout out to Spring '04 THE KOMISSION! YO!

Thank you to Michelle Spicely, who has been an angel in disguise. Michelle, you came along and offered a helping hand without asking for anything in return, and I could never repay you for the blessing you have been to the Xklusive Thoughts movement.

To the experts, Paul C. Brunson of **PaulCBrunson.com** and Stephan Labossiere of **StephanSpeaks.com**, who were the first ones willing to expose my work to the world by allowing me to write on their websites. You guys were leaders in the field and took a chance on me, and I am forever grateful.

To Lamar and Ronnie Tyler of **BlackAndMarriedWithKids.com**, thank you for seeing my potential and bringing me on as a staff writer. Thank you for being more than just employers, but for being mentors and being willing to share your knowledge and offer your insight and guidance. I have learned so much from you both, and I admire both of you as people and as experts in your field.

Finally, thank you to my audience who has followed me over the last few years. For every blog post you read, every tweet you retweet, every post or meme you share on Facebook, every event you attend, and every book you will buy, know that none of this would be possible without you. I learn more from you than you learn from me, and I appreciate all of the Xklusive Thoughts FAMILY. Special shout out to the #LTD family, you know who you are!

ABOUT THE AUTHOR

Troy Spry is a certified life and relationship coach and a Reality Expert. He is a graduate of Winthrop University where he studied psychology and officially began his lifelong study of human behavior. Troy founded the blog Xklusive Thoughts as a way to invite the world to share in the many interesting insights and conversations he has about life and love and the lessons they've taught him.

Troy has always been a talented writer and a "tell it like it is" friend to many seeking advice about relationships and life issues. He is known for his passion for helping people live life on purpose and for creating a positive narrative about relationships and marriage. This authenticity has made him a respected voice on the social media scene and an in-demand speaker at conferences and events.

Troy's popular blog, inspirational morning messages, lunchtime discussions, and personal one-on-one relationship and life coaching landed him a position as an official staff writer for the award-winning website *BlackAndMarriedWithKids.com*, where he was recently the recipient of the Writer's Choice Award. Troy also has had the pleasure of writing for celebrity matchmaker Paul C. Brunson, and he serves as a dating expert and contributor for *DatingAdvice.com* and *DigitalRomance.Com*.

Troy has been listed as a premier coach by *BlackMenRock.net* and had the honor of being a featured guest on HuffPost Live. Troy became an author with the publication of his first ebook, <u>Teach Me How to Love: A Man's Journey Toward and Through Marriage</u>.

Troy's mission is simple: to inspire individuals to first become better people so that they can become better mates, create better relationships, and ultimately help to build better communities. He is a firm believer in the philosophy that you must live life intentionally and on purpose!

Outside of his writing, coaching, and speaking endeavors, Troy enjoys playing sports, traveling, and spending time with his wife and friends. Troy's next big life challenge will be raising his new baby daughter. Time with those closest to him keeps him grounded, relatable, and humble.

You can contact and follow Troy on twitter and Instagram at **@Xklusive5** or on his Facebook fan page by searching **Xklusive Thoughts**. You can email him at **info@XklusiveThoughts.com**. Find out more about Troy by visiting his personal website and blog, **XklusiveThoughts.com**.

Sign up for Troy's email list on his website and you'll receive a free copy of his ebook, <u>Teach Me How to Love: A Man's Journey Toward and Through Marriage</u>.

REFERENCES

Carle, Gilda and Colette Bouchez, (2005), "Looking for Love: Understanding What You Need," WebMD June 7, 2015 http://www.webmd.com/sex-relationships/features/love-and-dating-what-you-need

Dictionary.com, (2015). Dictionary.com, LLC, 2015.

Furtick, Steven (2014), Elevation Church, as cited from a sermon.

Merriam-Webster, (2015). Merriam-Webster, Incorporated

White, JoAnne, "Looking for Love: Understanding What You Need. Define Your Core Values," WebMD June 7, 2015 http://www.webmd.com/sex-relationships/features/love-and-dating-what-you-need

Made in the USA
Lexington, KY
29 August 2018